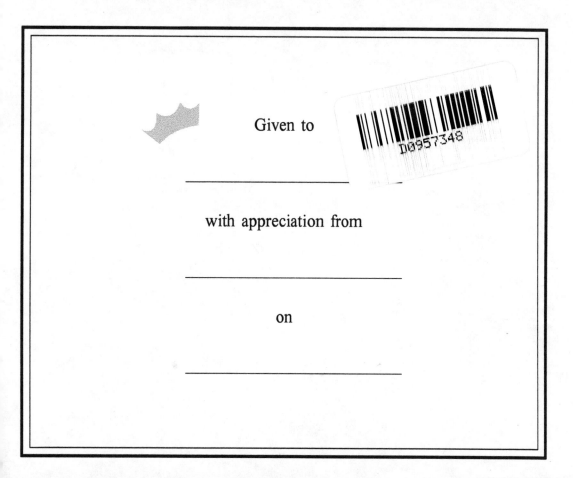

Given to

_____

with appreciation from

_____

on

_____

And now, friends, we ask you to honor those leaders who work so hard for you, who have been given the responsibility of urging and guiding you along in your obedience. Overwhelm them with appreciation and love!

1 Thessalonians 5:12-13, THE MESSAGE

ALL
PREACHERS
OF OUR
GOD & KING

Featuring stories by William Woughter
with quotations compiled by Keith Call

Harold Shaw Publishers
Wheaton, Illinois

Edited by Elizabeth Cody Newenhuyse

Designed by David LaPlaca

ISBN 0-87788-622-9

Library of Congress Cataloging-in-Publication Data

All preachers of our God and King / compiled by William Woughter and Keith Call.
    p. cm.
  ISBN 0-87788-622-9
  1. Clergy—Office—Quotations, maxims, etc. 2. Clergy—Anecdotes. 3. Clergy—Humor.
I. Woughter, William. II. Call, Keith.
BV660.2.A45 1997
253—dc21   97-15006
                                                  CIP

---

02 01 00 99 98 97

10 9 8 7 6 5 4 3 2 1

GOD'S
CALL

It seems so presumptuous, imperfect men and women responding to God with a "Here I am—send me!" Yet generation after generation of servants continue to commit their gifts and limitations to the service of Christ's work in the world. Here are a few stories and reflections on calls and beginnings and how God uses all we bring to him.

Is anyone?

The Reverend Ed Crandall told me a story about a Sunday when his district superintendent, the Reverend James Bence, was with them in a service. Bence sat down in the front pew with the Crandalls' young son, Steve, prior to the service. Bence was one to strike up conversations with children whenever possible, so he turned to the youngster and inquired, "Well, Steve, have you been a good boy lately?" To which Steve replied, "Yes."

Pushing his luck a little too far, the D.S. said, "Are you good all of the time?"

Steve looked him straight in the eye and shot back, "Well, are *you?*"

William Woughter

Fill in the blanks

[As I struggled with my] sense of call, I had about come to the conclusion that

I was not called to a ministry of writing and speaking, as I had thought, because the Lord did not seem to be blessing the work materially, and wasn't that a sign He wanted me to go do something else? I mean, how long do I have to wait on this, God? . . . [Over time I realized that] God wanted *me* to take responsibility, to understand that a call is not a blueprint. It's more of a rough outline that we're supposed to fill in. He's given us the freedom to work out the details.

Elizabeth Cody Newenhuyse, God, I Know You're Here Somewhere

Meaning and faithfulness

To stand at the doors of eternity is what God has asked Steve to do with his life. In answering and staying faithful to his call, he finds the meaning that originally propelled him into the ministry. Satisfaction has followed obedience.

David Goetz, "Why Pastor Steve Loves His Job," *Christianity Today*

Patching up the ordinand

The special night was almost upon us. I had worked hard and

long in preparation for my ordination into the Christian ministry. The ordination service for six other men and myself would take place the next night. We were seated in our church camp tabernacle on old wooden benches that had been nailed together by volunteers. I was dressed in the only suit I had and the seat of the pants was as thin as tissue. About six weeks before, I had ordered a new tailor-made suit. They had promised that it would be delivered in four weeks, but it had not arrived.

When the song leader said, with a wave of his hand, "Now on this last verse, let's all stand up and smile as we sing," I rose; and as I did so, I heard a terrible ripping sound. The whole seat of my pants had torn loose on a short nail head in the bench. My suit coat covered the situation . . . I hoped. At the end of the service, when the altar call was given, I slipped behind the nearby piano and "prayed" until everyone else had gone. The next day my wife and I went to town and bought what was then a new item, iron-on patches. My creative wife managed to get the seat back together and I never will know if anyone saw me "unseated" as I knelt before God at the ordination altar.

William Woughter

No blinking at Lincoln

There's a wonderful story told about Carl Sandburg that suggests what should be our response to God's revealed magnificence in Christ. Sandburg became so immersed in his study of Lincoln that he thought of little else. The people in the town where he studied and wrote decided to test his concentration on Abe with a practical joke. They noted that the historian went to breakfast at the same time and place each day. So they dressed up the tallest man in the town as Abraham Lincoln and had him walk down the street just in time to meet Sandburg as he walked to the restaurant. Everyone watched and listened as the two met. Without blinking an eye or slowing his pace, Sandburg tipped his hat and said, "Good morning, Mr. President," then went on to his breakfast. He was so engulfed in his Lincolnology that he was not surprised to see Lincoln on his own street!

The same thing happens to us in a much more significant way when we focus our thinking on the magnificence of God in Christ; we are not surprised when we meet Him face to face!

Lloyd John Ogilvie, Asking God Your Hardest Questions

But will predestination play in Peoria?
They debated zestfully now, here in the Pastry Shop, interrupting each other constantly and heaping their words together on the table. Jo, sipping her coffee, strained to follow them. "Decreed will of God," someone said, and "free play for the human will." Predestination. Determinism. If lives were predestined, or even foreknown, how did personal decisions matter a hill of beans? Did you really decide for Christ, or were you chosen to decide? They contended this, voices rising, until one of them (older than the others—at least he was quite

bald) cried out in despair, "But what shall I tell the little old ladies at South Podunk Baptist?" The others laughed and patted him on the shoulders. "Both truths, but not in the same sermon," someone answered.

Shirley Nelson, The Last Year of the War

Called to be cultivators
I believe that all believers, and especially ministers, should live with the profound sense of the responsibility to be cultivators, enabling others to be more than they deemed possible with the assistance of God's Spirit. Reflecting God's Word and God's perspective, Christian ministry is articulating the possibilities of God's love in every situation.

Janna Joy Roche, in a letter to her home church explaining her decision to enter the ministry; quoted by Leslie B. Flynn in *My Daughter a Preacher!?!*

More than Billy's son
I enjoy my life, even though there have been many moments of struggle and

pain. I share my life, not because I think there is anything particularly special about it, but because I want you to understand how great and capable God is of using anyone's life to accomplish His goals. If there's anything special about my story, it's not because I'm the son of Billy and Ruth Graham—it's because I'm a son of the living God.

Franklin Graham, Rebel with a Cause

Obeying the "Yield" sign

Obedience is the test of devotion. If we truly love our Lord we will be glad to yield all we are and have to Him for service. He has entrusted us who are saved with the message of His gospel. This does not mean that we are all called to be preachers or missionaries, but we are asked to confess Him before men that others may be drawn to Him as we have been. We shall find life at its richest and best if we yield to His call, no matter how great the cost may seem to be.

H. A. Ironside, The King's Couriers

Just say yes

Henri Nouwen on the tension between solitude with God and the demands of ministry: I'm like many pastors; I commit myself to projects and plans and then wonder how I can get them all done. This is true of the pastor, the teacher, the administrator. Indeed, it's true of our culture, which tells us, "Do as much as you can or you'll never make it." In that sense, pastors are part of the world. I've discovered I cannot fight the demons of busyness directly. I cannot continuously say no to this or no to that, unless there is something ten times more attractive to choose. Saying no to my lust, my greed, my needs, and the world's powers takes an enormous amount of energy.

The only hope is to find something so obviously real and attractive that I can devote all my energies to saying yes. One such thing I can say yes to is when I come in touch with the fact that . . . in my total brokenness I am still loved.

Quoted by Harold Myra in Leaders

Excuses, excuses

I believe that in *each generation* God has "called" enough men and women to evangelize all the yet unreached tribes of the earth. Why do I believe that? Because everywhere I go, I constantly meet with men and women who say to me, "When I was young I wanted to be a missionary, but I got married instead." Or, "My parents dissuaded me," or some such thing. No, it is not God who does not call. It is man who will not respond!

Isobel Kuhn, Nests above the Abyss

Bzzz

Having lived in South America as missionaries, my family and I realized that moving to another jungle location meant a lot of work. We knew the discomforts of such things as snakes and bugs.

One morning, a few days after beginning to clean our temporary home, the family and I were taking a short break. While we were drinking tea, a large black beetle suddenly flew through the room with a loud buzzing noise. As it darted between us, my wife let out a startled scream.

Astonished more by her scream than the beetle, my youngest daughter cried out, "For heaven's sake, Mom!"

My wife resolutely replied, "That's the only reason I'm here."

Patrick Jenkins, Humor for Preaching & Teaching

Satan's target

When you are doing what Jesus Christ has called you to do, you can count on two things: You will possess spiritual power because you have the presence of Christ, and you'll experience opposition because the Devil does not concentrate on secondary targets. He never majors on the minors.

Neither should we.

Howard Hendricks, Leaders

For your soul only

There are strands of the call of God providentially at work that you know and no one else does. It is the threading of God's voice for you on some particular line, and it is no use to consult anyone else about it, or to say that other people are dull because they do not hear it.

Oswald Chambers

Or try faxing

Many years ago when my brothers were small, one of them said to the other, "I'm going to eat you!"

My mother overheard and said, "Oh, we don't eat people. There are some people who eat other people. We call them cannibals. Someone should tell them about Jesus."

To which David replied, "Well, they'd better tell them over the telephone."

Miriam Martin, Humor for Preaching & Teaching

Holy abandon

It is bats that are supposed to be found in belfries, but for a few incandescent moments in 1831 a man named Lyman Woodard was to be found in one that is still higher than any other building in Rupert, Vermont. The event is described in its proper place. Suffice it to say here only that one day he climbed up and stood on his head in that belfry. Why did he do it? Was he drunk? Was he crazy? Who knows? Who even cares? The point is that it was a gorgeous, clownish, inspired, and inspiring thing to do. It was a radically new way of looking at the mysteries of earth and heaven. It is Saint Paul writing, "We are fools for Christ's sake." It is David dancing naked before the ark. It is the rapturous shenanigans and holy abandon of faith kicking up its heels and considering the lilies of the field from an altogether different vantage.

Frederick Buechner, The Clown in the Belfry

Where ministry begins

The next clearest satisfaction to knowing what you can do is knowing what you can't do. After some private travail, I'm happy to state that I'll never preach to multitudes or build cathedrals or translate scriptures or sing and dance in videos.

But this I own: I can take your hand and look you in the eye and ask, "How are you?" and mean it and know that here is where we both belong. Now begins ministry, serious and eternal.

A. J. Webb

People and places
The answer to most problems is the right people in the right places.

Fred Smith

No one's *that* important
One of the best bloopers I ever heard occurred one Sunday when our rather pompous minister was telling a story about himself. He meant to say, "Back when I was a child," but he actually said, "Back when I was God." It was a beautiful Freudian slip that fit the man perfectly. It was also on a live radio broadcast.

Donald Cooper, as quoted in *Once Upon a Pew*, compiled by Ken Alley

Something great and mysterious

Jan Karon, author of the Mitford stories, on her conversion:

"There were no visions at the foot of my bed. There were no bolts of lightning. . . . As time went on I began to see very clearly that something great had happened that was far too mysterious for me to understand."

Publisher's Weekly

GOD'S WORK
☙

There are times when "God's work" really lives up to the name—when we baptize a new believer, when we look out at the congregation and realize that the sermon is connecting, when we sit quietly with a saint who is dying.

There are other times when "God's work" is somewhat less awesome, when it's funny or mundane or thought-provoking.

First time for everything?

Shortly after his very first worship service at his first pastorate, the Rev. Ed Crandall was approached by a young couple who requested that he officiate at their wedding. The new and youthful pastor replied, "Well, I will do my best, but remember, this is my very first marriage."

"That's all right," the groom reassured him. "This is my first one, too."

William Woughter

The purpose

This ministry is a center for spiritual growth,
where positive attitudes are developed,
where good people become better,
where hurts are healed,
where lessons are learned,

where friendships are developed,

where marriages are strengthened,

where families are bonded,

where the restless find peace,

where love is alive,

where God is understood,

where Jesus Christ is Lord.

Crystal Cathedral Ministries Statement of Purpose and Mission

Resting in the Rock

Life should be deeply laid in its bases, strongly cemented together in its principles, noble in its convictions; then it can be charitable in its concessions and recognitions. On what is your life based? What is the point at which you are aiming? If you have no broad foundation, no solid rock, no complete purpose and policy, then you are adventurers, speculators, and the turn of the wheel will mean your present or ultimate ruin.

Joseph Parker, The People's Bible

Monks at play

What sets monks apart from the rest of us is not an overbearing piety but a contemplative sense of fun. They know, as Trappist monk Matthew Kelty reminds us, that "you do not have to be holy to love God. You have only to be human. Nor do you have to be holy to see God in all things. You have only to play as a child with an unselfish heart." The play of monks comes out of . . . the humble acknowledgment that, for them, the liturgy must be a daily affair. . . . They need to act it out, . . . singing and saying and hearing the words again and again, as a child asks to hear a beloved story many times over.

Kathleen Norris, Dakota: A Spiritual Geography

Complete, don't compete

There are pastors who use the church as a platform to launch a personal significance campaign. They do battle with deacons, elders, and charter members who also want to use the church to enhance their power and position. . . . This obsessive pursuit obstructs authentic Christian living. Our obsession with significance stimulates things that are counter to the values and behavior of those who follow Christ. Authentic Christianity does not call for defensive responses, but a vulnerable spirit that we might be taught by the Spirit. . . . True Christianity calls us to complement one another, not to compete.

Joseph M. Stowell, Perilous Pursuits

Cornmeal and spiritual truth

Dad . . . did not preach in that stilted and perfunctory manner so common to those of the cloth. He did not indulge in highbrow dissertations about abstract ideas. He was a lay person, chatting with lay people, about the character and conduct of his closest friend, the living Christ. . . .

Whenever he spoke to the Africans, he used parables just as Jesus did. He couched his remarks in vivid word pictures that were readily grasped and long remembered. He spoke much of water, grain, seed, soil, sheep, and cornmeal. These were the languages of the land but also the stepping stones that led the soul to lay hold of a spiritual truth.

W. Philip Keller, Chosen Vessels

Drama through the tedium

I was startled one day by a casual observation made by Billy Graham. He said he felt his "real gift" was writing his fundraising letters. The statement caught me off guard. What did he mean? He wasn't denigrating his preaching, although it's well known that he refers to himself as a simple country preacher. He was simply sensing the importance of a personal gift easily undervalued. He cares deeply about those letters that carry his name and share his heart and concerns with his supporters. That's a vital part of his leadership, as is his voluminous personal correspondence, which may often feel to him like a mundane burden.

We all get involved with menial functions, correspondence among them. Yet the sense of God's call and the drama of our gifts being used can give even correspondence and tedious desk work a value that goes beyond our feelings and perceptions.

Harold Myra, Leaders

The grind of the machine

Now that same day was Religion day, and not a few of the clergy, always glad to seize on any passing event to give interest to the dull and monotonic grind of their intellectual machines, made this remarkable one the ground of discourse to their congregations.

George MacDonald, The Princess and Curdie

How lives are touched

I've been a pastor's wife. I know how few strokes ministers can get from "their" people, except maybe at the farewell testimonial banquet. Sometimes pastors, especially on those days of tedium, wonder if they're making a difference, seeing the fruit of changed lives.

As someone who has been touched by the ministry of several pastors, I think that part of the problem is that the fruit isn't always dramatically visible. Lives change incrementally; the John Newton-style conversion is pretty much the exception in the local church. Pastors often touch people in smaller, though no less significant, ways, and these changes add up over time. Here I want to acknowledge a few of the shepherds who made a difference in me:

Mr. C.: You left us way, way too soon, which may be why you've taken on a saintly aura in my mind. I remember you leading my confirmation class. I don't remember much of what you taught, but I remember your gentleness and godliness and the feeling you gave me of a man set apart by God. It would take years, but your model helped lead me to the Lord.

Charlie: You never got swallowed up in the pastoral identity—in other words, you stayed real and had a life outside the church. I liked how you would go home and play with your dog and watch sports and laugh with your wife. I guess you could call it balance.

Dave: I know you had your detractors in the church. We weren't among them.

I loved your sermons, always rich with applicable ideas on living the Christian life. I still think you're one of the best preachers I've ever heard.

Greg I: I'm only now beginning to see how your personal pain at a young age deepened your ministry and made you so much more than "the youth guy." You showed me how spiritual growth can come out of the fruitful tension between humanness and holiness.

Greg II: I heard you preach once; I would like to again. Months later several of your images and insights have stuck. Please hang in—you have a real gift.

Lydia Lee Reynolds

Are you a known Clivaholic?

Have you ever noticed church phenomena for which there should be a term, yet none exists? No longer. Introducing . . . *The Living Lexicon: Church Terms That Oughta Be.*

Biblidue: The build-up of bookmarks, bulletins, notes, and other miscellanea that collects in one's Bible.

Clivaholic: One who can no longer control the compulsion to quote C. S. Lewis in every sermon, lesson, or conversation.

Pewtrify: To occupy a precise spot in the sanctuary for more than fifteen years without ever showing signs of sentient life.

Deaconscript: An unwilling church officer cajoled into a position of leadership.

Hymnprovisation: The abrupt and unannounced transition from one song to another, usually a chorus unfamiliar to most present.

Rob Suggs, Humor for Preaching & Teaching

Ritual lite

The wedding ceremony started out well and pastor Jerry Jack expected no problems. Then the groom became exceedingly nervous and his teeth started chattering loudly—so loudly that he couldn't talk and the ceremony had to be delayed for two hours.

Fortunately Jack remembered that his denomination's book of worship included a wedding service that took only two minutes. They managed to get the groom calmed down long enough to get through the briefest ceremony the pastor ever conducted.

Let's hope it wasn't an omen for the marriage.

William Woughter

Job description

The Country Parson hath a special care of his Church, that all things there be decent, and befitting his Name by which it is called. Therefore first he takes order, that all things be in good repair, as walls plastered, windows glazed, floor paved, seats whole, firm, and uniform, especially that the Pulpit, and Desk, and Communion Table, and font be as they ought, for those great duties that are performed in them. Secondly, that the Church be swept, and kept clean without dust, or Cobwebs, and at great festivals strawed, and stuck with boughs, and perfumed with incense. Thirdly, that there be fit, and proper texts of Scripture everywhere painted, and that all the painting be grave, and reverend, not with light colors, or foolish antics.

George Herbert, The Country Parson

Job description, II

Some kids' definitions of a pastor:

He works for God.

He wrote the Bible.

He's the bald guy that sings real loud.

Pastors make my mom happy and my dad mad.

Pastors eat a lot at picnics.

They talk a long time about stuff.

They go to church all the time.

He gets all the money in the plates.

He's the guy that works at the church with the janitor.

Bob Simon, quoted in *Once Upon a Pew,* compiled by Ken Alley

Ministering or performing?

None of us is immune to putting ourselves first. I don't think I've learned anything about myself that has more surprised and appalled me than how reflexively I put my own needs first.

[When I spoke at my brother's memorial service], at one point during my talk, I noticed that a phrase I had just used was especially rich. As any experienced public speaker might do, I paused to let that phrase sink in. During that three-second pause, I heard these words run through my mind, *I'm doing a pretty good job. That was a good pause.* Immediately, I felt slapped in the face by the realization that at that moment I cared more about how I was performing than about how meaningfully I was ministering. . . .

[Yet] God's grace frees me *from* needing to be better than I am and frees me to face what I'm really like without giving up. The shock of seeing the truth about myself enables me to embrace God's grace more fully.

Larry Crabb, Finding God

Show us the man on the Cross!

I once heard one of the greatest chaplains the British Army ever had tell a story about that great soldier Field Marshal Slim. The thing happened in the Burma campaign. Slim asked the senior chaplain to arrange for a visit to one of his soldiers who was going through a bad time. News had come to Burma that his wife was behaving, to say the least of it, indiscreetly at home. The chaplain was duly sent to see the man. After the visit Slim sent for the senior chaplain. "Padre," he said, "about that visit I asked you to get one of your chaplains to pay." "Well, sir," said the senior chaplain, "what about it?" "Well, padre," said Slim, "your chaplain went to see the man. He was very nice to him. He smoked a cigarette with him, and drank a cup of tea with him. But he never showed that soldier the one thing he wanted to see." "What was that?" said the senior chaplain. And Slim answered: "The man on the Cross."

William Barclay, A Spiritual Autobiography

Total immersion

In 1950 [in] Osaka, Japan, I was the guest of a distinguished Christian businessman and his family. It was a hot summer night. The host had slid open the bamboo doors and walls so that evening breezes could circulate and cool his lovely Japanese home. The family decided to treat me to a traditional Japanese bath. A fire was lit beneath a great iron tub. I had seen others enter those steaming cauldrons only to emerge moments later looking lobster-red and wrinkled. The family gathered at a nearby table for tea and sweet desserts.

"Aren't you going to undress and get in while it's still nice and hot?" my host asked in perfect though accented English.

"I can't undress here," I whispered, "not in front of your whole family."

For a moment, that dear man looked confused. Then he smiled, pulled several wall partitions in place and turned politely aside. The partition had large, uncovered spaces through which I could see the family and they could see me. Hoping to offend no one, I hung the giant bath towel over the partition, undressed quickly and was about to climb into the tub when the wife of my host walked directly up to me and asked politely, "Would you like some soap?"

I was a Baptist preacher from Dallas, Texas, and there I stood, stark naked, before that beautiful and innocent Japanese mother.

"Thank you," I mumbled, grasping the soap and noticing for the first time that when I really blush, I blush all over!

W. A. Criswell, Standing on the Promises

Do you want to be like Chuck?

[If you want to find your niche] you shouldn't listen to Charles Swindoll and say, "I'm going to be like him," if you don't have his abilities. Despite his dedication to extensive study and prayer, he has the ability to see the helpful things we often miss, and he can communicate truth in memorable ways. . . .

You shouldn't pick a model and say, "He's interesting; he has a following; I want to be like him." You need to say, "God, what are my gifts? Help me to see what they are, and help me to develop them to the best of my ability." That may mean that you will have fewer followers than other leaders, but the followers you have will be the ones God wants you to have.

J. Richard Chase, Leaders

What Chuck does

I'll let you in on my own experience—the trap I fell into years ago. Having been exposed to a few of the "greats" in various churches and an outstanding seminary, I (like some of the other guys in the class) tried to be like *them.* You know, think like, sound like, look like. For over ten years in the ministry I—a rabbit—worked hard at swimming like a duck or flying like an eagle. I was a frustrated composite creature . . . like that weird beast in the second chapter of Daniel. And my feet of clay were slowly crumbling beneath me. It was awful! The worst part of all, what little bit of originality or creativity I had was being consumed in that false role I was forcing. One day my insightful and caring wife asked me, "Why not just be *you?* Why try to be like anybody else?" Well, friends and neighbors, this rabbit quit the swim team and gave up flying lessons and stopped trying to climb. Talk about relief! And best of all, I learned it was

OK to be me . . . and let my family members be themselves. Originality and creativity flowed anew!

Charles Swindoll, Growing Strong in the Seasons of Life

Record-breaking events

My wife, Marge, and I still laugh about it when we think of a ridiculous situation I got myself into. Many years ago, in a Sunday school contest in our church in Bentley Creek, Pennsylvania, I came up with an idea for a Sunday school record-breaking contest. Back in those days the phonograph records were made of a waxy material and were easily broken. We took five old records and painted on each one the attendance number that we hoped to break that coming Sunday. I boldly announced that the person who brought in the most visitors during the next five weeks would have the privilege of breaking the last record over my head.

We broke the attendance records, as we had hoped, every Sunday, and on the last Sunday went far beyond our wildest dreams. Over that period one young boy had brought in twenty-seven visitors. He proudly marched to the front of the church, took the final record and whacked me over the head.

Much to my consternation, the record did not break, nor did it break during the subsequent thumps on my head. We then discovered that this last record had been produced with a metal core. I don't remember how we fulfilled the promise to the boy, but I do remember my sore head.

William Woughter

War stories

When you serve in one place for several years, you develop a depth of friendships that few other people know. I pastored one church for fifteen years, and on my last Sunday there we had Communion. As I handed the plate to those twelve men lined up before the congregation and looked each of them in the eye, I realized there was some secret between me and every one of them. . . . [The] feeling had been almost like going through war together. The secret bound our lives inextricably together.

Jay Kesler, Being Holy, Being Human

GOD'S WORD

G eorge MacDonald has been quoted as saying that if a person feels it is easy to tell the truth, that person has never tried. Maybe that's why preaching—which, at its heart, is telling the Truth—can seem such an awesome task. Pastors are lower-case humans sharing news of an uppercase God, and so, at times, humorous and humbling things happen. At other times we can almost see the dry bones stand up and dance.

To the right

Stay true to what is right, and God will save you and those who hear you.

1 Timothy 4:16, NLT

Preaching about God vs. preaching God

And what is the shape of so much preaching today? Why, it is the shape of the classroom: teaching. And teaching is always (in our consideration) one step removed from experience and from the "real." It is an activity of the mind. . . . The God who is met in doctrines, who is apprehended in the catechesis, who is true so long as our statements *about* him are truly stated, who is communicated in propositions, premise-premise-conclusion, who leaps not from the streets, nor even from scriptural texts, but from the *interpretation* of the scriptural texts— that God is an abstract, has been abstracted from the rest of the Christian's experience.

Walter Wangerin, Jr., Ragman and Other Cries of Faith

Take and drink

Biblical metaphors—*panting* after God, *tasting* God, *drinking* living water, *eating* bread from heaven—make it clear that finding God is not merely academic. We are to do more than understand truth about God; we are to encounter him, as a bride encounters her husband on their wedding night. Finding God is a sensual experience.

Larry Crabb, Finding God

Amen, brother! Don't preach it!

One of our closest friends in our early years was the daughter of a woman who was very involved in the Salvation Army. Edna's mother distributed the *War Cry,* worked in the Army's store, and, of course, attended every worship service.

As a child, Edna became very weary during some of the services. Her mother remembered one sermon during which Edna kept saying, "Amen! Amen!" Her mother tried to hush

her, but it happened several times during the service. At the end
Edna said to her mother, "I kept saying 'Amen,' but that man
would *not* stop talking."

William Woughter

No doubt?

If the congregation is saying, "What a beautiful! faith our pastor has. He has no
doubts in the world," then we, and they, are in serious trouble.

Jay Kesler, Being Holy, Being Human

Christ's trumpet

[My friend] A. J. Gossip lived closer to God than any man I have ever known.
At one time he was minister of St Matthew's in Glasgow. I have heard him tell
how there was a week when pressure of all kinds of things made it difficult to
make the preparation he knew he should have made. "You know the stair up to
the pulpit in St Matthew's?" he said. "You know the bend on the stair? Jesus

Christ met me there. I saw him as clearly as I see you. He looked at the sermon in my hand. 'Gossip,' he said to me, 'is this the best you could do for me this week?'" and Gossip went on: "Thinking back over the business of that week, I could honestly say, 'Yes, Lord, it is my best.'" And said Gossip: "Jesus Christ took that poor thing that Sunday morning and in his hands it became a trumpet."

William Barclay, a Spiritual Autobiography

The botheration of it all!

[Though] I liked clergymen as I liked bears, I had as little wish to be in the Church as in the zoo. It was, to begin with, a kind of collective; a wearisome "get-together" affair. I couldn't yet see how a concern of that sort should have anything to do with one's spiritual life. To me, religion ought to have been a matter of good men praying alone and meeting by twos and threes to talk of spiritual matters. And then the fussy, time-wasting botheration of it all! the bells, the crowds, the umbrellas, the notices, the bustle, the perpetual arranging and organizing. Hymns were (and are) extremely disagreeable to me. Of all musical instruments I liked (and like) the organ least.

C. S. Lewis, Surprised by Joy

The public duties of the Congregation

The Country Parson, as soon as he awakes on Sunday morning, presently falls to work, and seems to himself so as a Marketman is, when the Market day comes, or a shopkeeper, when customers use to come in. His thoughts are full of making the best of the day, and contriving it to his best gains. . . . [When] the hour calls, with his family attending him, he goes to Church, at his first entrance *humbly adoring, and worshipping the invisible majesty, and presence of Almighty God,* and blessing the people either openly, or to himself. Then having read divine Service twice fully, and preached in the morning, and catechized in the afternoon, he thinks he hath in some measure, according to poor, and frail man, discharged the public duties of the Congregation.

George Herbert, The Country Parson

Things pondered during dry sermons

- Why does the preacher always get long-winded on the Sunday you need to be somewhere else by noon?
- I wonder if anyone has ever poured bubble bath in the baptistry?
- Funny how people scramble to get a front seat at the ballpark, but grab a back seat at church.
- If you don't feel as close to God as you once did, who moved?
- If Jesus had been stoned to death, would Catholics have to hit themselves instead of making the sign of the Cross?
- I'm so tired of those sermons on patience!

Ken Alley, P.K., Once Upon a Pew

Cassocks on hassocks

Remarkable are the forms which pulpits have assumed according to the freaks of human fancy and folly. Twenty years ago they had probably reached their very worst. What could have been their design and intent it would be hard to conjecture. A deep wooden pulpit of the old sort might well remind a minister of his mortality, for it is nothing but a coffin set on end: but on what rational ground do we bury our pastors alive? . . .

No one knows the discomfort of pulpits except the man who has been in very many, and found each one worse than the last. They are generally so deep that a short person like myself can scarcely see over the top of them, and when I ask for something to stand upon they bring me a hassock. . . . It is too much to expect us to keep the balance of our minds and the equilibrium of our bodies at the same time. The tippings up, and overturnings of stools and hassocks which I have had to suffer while preaching rush on my memory now, and revive the most painful sensations. . . . We ought to rise superior to such trifles, but though the spirit truly is willing the flesh is weak.

C. H. Spurgeon, Letters to My Students

But what does the Greek say?
One Sunday morning the pastor read John 14:2 to the congregation using a

modern translation. His version read, "In my Father's house there are many dwelling places."

Immediately an elderly lady stood up and said, "I want you to read that Scripture again—from my Bible. I've lived in old, run-down houses all my life, and I'm looking forward to that mansion!"

Carol Reddekop, Humor for Preaching & Teaching

Communing with the Word

No man can doubt the inspiration of the Bible who has read it—not galloped through it, but sat down with it, talked with it, communed with it, till his heart burned within him, and until the heavens touched the earth in condescending love, and earth bloomed with heaven's summer because of its access of light.

Joseph Parker, The People's Bible

Devoted to study

We come to Scripture to be changed, not to amass information.

We must understand, however, that a vast difference exists between the study of Scripture and the devotional reading of Scripture. In the study of Scripture a high priority is placed upon interpretation: what it means. In the devotional reading of Scripture a high priority is placed upon application: what it means for me. All too often people rush to the application stage and bypass the interpretation stage: they want to know what it means for them before they know what it means!

Richard Foster, Celebration of Discipline

The Well

Drink from the Well, not from the streams that flow from the Well.

Amy Carmichael, Whispers of His Power

Beyond the fellow struggler

It does no good merely to illustrate our imperfection and leave it at that. Most of our people know we're imperfect already. What they need to hear is our desire to honor God in this situation.

One pastor I know has built a strong and vibrant church, and one of his secrets has been taking the "fellow struggler" stance with the congregation. He respects the people enough to be honest with them. . . .

Without fear, he'll occasionally get up in the pulpit and say, "I've been trying this particular approach to Bible study, and it's not working." Or, "I find it hard to maintain myself in prayer; I go to sleep, or my thoughts stray. But I'm determined not to give up. Recently I've begun to write down my prayers, and I try to pray one good, short prayer rather than a long, impressive one."

He's been honest with people; he's shared his struggle. But in the process he has been leading his people, not dragging them down.

Jay Kesler, Being Holy, Being Human

I know an old lady who swallowed a . . .

I was pastoring a Wesleyan church in Bentley Creek, Pennsylvania. The church had been built out of material from a large, old home and in the springtime was infested with flies and hornets. The church janitor had done everything possible to kill the critters, but they still plagued the building.

During one of my sermons I opened my mouth—and in flew a half-crazed fly. I couldn't do anything but gag and was forced to swallow the fly. My sympathetic congregation was relieved when I recovered and said, "That reminds me of the scripture, 'I was a stranger and you took me in.' "

William Woughter

Charles Spurgeon, critic

We know Spurgeon as one of the great nineteenth-century preachers. But he was also a pithy critic. Here he assesses several commentaries on the Book of Job:

On Gregory the Great's commentary: The Fathers are of course beyond criticism, and contain priceless gems here and there; but they spiritualize at such a rate, and also utter so many crudities and platitudes, that if they were modern writers they would not be so greatly valued as they are. Antiquity lends enchantment.

On a book on Elihu, written by one Walter Hodges: Based upon the absurd supposition that Elihu was the Son of God himself, and Job a type of the Saviour. Poor Job's book has been the subject of trials as numerous as those of its hero, and Hodges has given the finishing stroke. The course of dreaming can no further go.

On an effort to "update" Job as a modern poem: This will hardly do. . .

C. H. *Spurgeon,* Commenting & Commentaries

God's truth

When two truths seem to directly oppose each other, we must not question either, but remember there is a third—God—who reserves to himself the right to harmonize them.

Madame Anne Soymanov Swetchine

And you thought turkeys were dumb

The last church I served as minister before retirement was a church called Buena Vista, located in a rural area near Bath, New York. For many years they have had a wonderful yearly celebration called "Harvest Day." The pastor was not allowed to see the church until Harvest Day Sunday morning. At that time he would see the entire front of the church arrayed in the bounty of the harvest given for his family's benefit.

There is living not too far from the church a man with a twinkle in his eye and a sharp sense of humor. His name is Dean Stewart. One year he told the committee, "I'll donate a turkey if you'll let me put it in a cage where it can see and be seen by all."

When Harvest Day arrived, there was the bird, right up front, just as Stewart had promised. The turkey made some noise during the opening parts of the service, but when I started to preach its gobbling made a dreadful racket. After the noise became really annoying, I looked right at the bird and said, "If you don't stop that noise I will make you preach the rest of this sermon."

From that point on, the turkey was completely silent.

William Woughter

GOD'S SERVANT ❦

Who the pastor is . . . who others expect him or her to be . . . what pastors expect of themselves . . . what God requires of the pastor. Out of these challenges come blessings and tensions, humor and growth.

Scary thought

One morning I thought, *What if today I were a pastor instead of a corporation president?* That idea scared me to death.

Fred Smith, Leaders

And the leader is . . .

A leader must be well-thought-of, committed to his wife, cool and collected, accessible, and hospitable. He must know what he's talking about, not be over-fond of wine, not pushy but gentle, not thin-skinned, not money-hungry. He must handle his own affairs well, attentive to his own children and having their respect. For if someone is unable to handle his own affairs, how can he take care of God's church?

1 Timothy 3:1-5, THE MESSAGE

 Contagious faith

You have to admire a person who cares a great deal about her pastor's health, but this one seemed a little far out. When I was pastoring a new church in Kalamazoo, Michigan, I got a phone call from a lady. She said, "Pastor Woughter, I got your name from a relative of mine who attends your church. I wonder if I can ask you to do a favor for me." I told her I would be glad to if I could. She continued, "My father is in the hospital with a very communicable disease and we do not want our pastor to catch it. Would you please go to the hospital and pray with my father?" I did and am here to tell the story, thanks to the Lord.

William Woughter

And your Father who sees in secret . . .

Hidden, anonymous ministries affect even people who know nothing of them. They sense a deeper love and compassion among people though they cannot account for the feeling. If a secret service is done on their behalf, they are inspired to deeper devotion, for they know that the well of service is far deeper than they can see. It is a ministry that can be engaged in frequently by all people. It sends ripples of joy and celebration through any community of people.

Richard Foster, Celebration of Discipline

"Is it you again?"

A story said to originate in a Russian Orthodox monastery has an older monk telling a younger one: "I have finally learned to accept people as they are. Whatever they are in the world, a prostitute, a prime minister, it is all the same to me. But sometimes I see a stranger coming up the road and I say, 'Oh, Jesus Christ, is it you again?'"

Kathleen Norris, Dakota: A Spiritual Geography

The deputy

A Pastor is the Deputy of Christ for the reducing of Man to the Obedience of God.

George Herbert, The Country Parson

Grunts, groans, and grace

After lunch we celebrated a special Eucharist for Adam, the young man [Henri] Nouwen looked after. With solemnity, but also a twinkle in his eye, Nouwen led the liturgy in honor of Adam's twenty-sixth birthday. Unable to talk, walk, or dress himself, profoundly retarded, Adam gave no sign of comprehension. He seemed to recognize, at least, that his family had come. He drooled throughout the ceremony and grunted loudly a few times.

Later Nouwen told me it took him nearly two hours to prepare Adam each day, . . . [and] I must admit I had a fleeting doubt as to whether this was the best use of the busy priest's time. Could not someone else take over the manual chores? . . . But [Nouwen told me] he had learned to love Adam, truly to love him. In the process he had learned what it must be like for God to love us— spiritually uncoordinated, retarded, able to respond with what must seem to God like inarticulate grunts and groans.

Philip Yancey, "The Holy Inefficiency of Henri Nouwen," *Christianity Today*

Hallowed be the mundane

Sad to say, the people who seem to lose touch with themselves and with God most conspicuously are of all things ministers. As a minister myself I am peculiarly aware of this. . . .

Ministers run the awful risk, in other words, of ceasing to be witnesses to the presence in their own lives—let alone in the lives of the people they are trying to minister to—of a living God who transcends everything they think they know and can say about him and is full of extraordinary surprises. . . .

I believe that we are called to see that the day-to-day lives of all of us—the things that happened long ago, the things that happened only this morning—are also hallowed and crucial and part of a great drama in which souls are lost and souls are saved including our own.

Frederick Buechner, Telling Secrets

You know you're having a bad day when . . .

- In the pulpit you notice your sermon notes this week are for last week's sermon.
- The youth pastor urgently asks you about the church's liability insurance.
- You can't find Obadiah in a Bible study.
- You finally remember the name of that person you promised to visit in the hospital—while reading the obituaries.
- You are informed that the youth group used steel sponges for their car wash.
- You are elected pastor emeritus—and you're only twenty-eight.

  James D. Berkley, Humor for Preaching & Teaching

An offer you can refuse

A radio host recently asked the guest for that day what she thought would be a wonderful way to minister to the pastor's wife. "Maybe offer to clean house for her, or something like that?" he said. The cows will come home before a pastor's wife wants a church member digging socks (and who knows what else) out from under her kids' beds.

Wendy Murray Zoba, "What Pastors' Wives Wish Their Husbands Knew," *Christianity Today*

Not so small
Small things done with great love can change the world.

Steve Sjogren, Servant Warfare

The subtlest temptation
Screwtape to Wormwood:

What you want [in tempting the new Christian] is to keep a sly self-congratulation mixing with all his thoughts and never allow him to raise the question "What, precisely, am I congratulating myself *about?*" The idea of belonging to an inner ring, of being in a secret, is very sweet to him. Play on that nerve.

C. S. Lewis, The Screwtape Letters

The pastor and the poor

The Country Parson owing a debt of Charity to the poor, and of Courtesy to his other parishioners, he so distinguisheth, that he keeps his money for the poor, and his table for those that are above Alms. Not but that the poor are welcome also to his table, whom he sometimes purposely takes home with him, setting them close by him, and carving for them, both for his own humility, and their comfort, who are much cheered with such friendlinesses.

George Herbert, The Country Parson

Too much of a good thing

A pastor friend told me of an incident that caused him some grief while he was an evangelist at a Wesleyan camp.

He knew several people at the camp, and one couple had invited him out for an early evening meal. That had slipped his mind when he accepted an invitation from another couple for the midday meal—that same day. "We want to take you to a very special restaurant," they said. "We want you to get anything you want, regardless of the price. There's a special dessert we insist you try." The restaurant was very plush, and the evangelist stuffed himself accordingly, special dessert and all.

He had not been back at the camp workers' cottage very long when along came the second couple, ready to go out to eat. It was only then that he remembered their invitation and went along—to, you guessed it, "a very special restaurant, with a special dessert to try."

They had the same waitress, and she looked at him strangely as he tried to order as little as possible without offending his hosts. He hoped the waitress would think he was an identical twin. He hoped she wouldn't say anything. She didn't, but he never felt so stuffed and miserable in his life. (He didn't tell me whether he began writing down all his appointments after that day.)

William Woughter

A glorious indifference to credentials

We hear a lot of talk in the church today about people being able to use their gifts, about green-yellow-red lights, about folks fitting into exactly the right slots. It all makes sense in the creation of an effective organization.

But is "effectiveness" part of the church's mission? Recently it has occurred to me that while God welcomes all service, He is especially pleased by our doing the hard thing, the help we don't have time to give but manage to do anyway, the action that goes against our grain.

Certainly a church shouldn't make a practice of placing people in positions they're totally unqualified for (me on the Trustee Board, for example). And yes, it's a joy to see native abilities nurtured and honed. Still, I wonder if part of the church's glory, and part of what makes the church stand apart from the world, shines from its—ours, God's—cheerful indifference to credentials. Here is where the overloaded professional woman can take time to make a meal for a family coping with flood damage; where the blue-collar retiree can read to the preschool class; where the teenage athletic standout can help plan a worship service.

All this may smack of "Hey, let's put on a church in the barn!" amateurish enthusiasm. But where else will people have a chance to try, stretch, grow—and occasionally fail—for the sake of the Kingdom?

Lydia Lee Reynolds

Difficult, exhausting, satisfying

I began by being the pastor of a congregation. I can honestly say that that part of my work was the most difficult and exhausting that I ever had to do, and at the same time the most satisfying, even if it was also the most humiliating in that it could have been done so very much better.

William Barclay, A Spiritual Autobiography

And sometimes embarrassing

Dr. John White, president of Geneva College in western Pennsylvania, was invited to bring the message on Sunday morning in an evangelical Presbyterian church. The church had been built in a very avant-garde architectural style, different from any he had seen before. The pastor was not there and had left no instructions or anyone to give instructions. Here's what happened:

White could not find his seat and was forced to ask one of the choir members.

He could not find the responsive reading he was to lead. (The readings were in the center of the hymnal, instead of the back.)

He could not find the offering plates in the communion table. Worse, he was dressed in a clerical robe, which he wasn't used to, and said he felt like a "wounded bird" flailing about looking for the plates.

"The amazing thing is, they still invited me back," White marveled later.

William Woughter

"When the clock strikes for me . . ."

So much did Peter love to preach, so sure was he that this was the thing God had designed him to do, that it was hard for him to turn down engagements. Though he had a rugged constitution—for Scotland's rigorous climate does not pamper its people—his strength did not quite equal his enthusiasm. On the morning of March 31, 1946, he collapsed in the pulpit with an attack of coronary thrombosis. After a few months of convalescence, he launched into the most vigorous and productive period of his life. Then [at the age of forty-six] on January 25, 1949 at 8:15 in the morning, quietly he slipped through those phantom walls that separate this life from the next. We had only five hours' warning.

"When the clock strikes for me," he had said, "I shall go, not one minute early, and not one minute late. Until then, there is nothing to fear. I know that the promises of God are true, for they have been fulfilled in my life time and time again. Jesus still teaches and guides and protects and heals and comforts, and still wins our complete trust and our love.

"The measure of a life, after all, is not its duration, but its donation."

Catherine Marshall, The Best of Peter Marshall

Are we ready for wonder?

Few of us stand, on any given day, equipped for tragedy. Few of us are ready for grief so profound we can no longer even feel our way into the wet, gray haze of the future.

I have learned, though, that few of us are any better braced for magnificence. In the average course of the average day, few of us are really prepared for the wonder left strewn behind mystery, shimmering on the wake of a miracle.

So childbirth took me by surprise.

I have learned that there is sometimes wonder waiting—even for the unprepared.

I have learned that there are moments in human existence in which worship burns in our very bones, in which our spirits tremble and our reason quakes as we glimpse the molten center of life. For new body draws new breath the moment pain gives way to power. The two shall become one and one shall become two and strength is made perfect in weakness: I tell you a mystery. We have grasped the hand of God this day and found language insufficient, save one word only: *Yes*.

Joy Jordan-Lake, Grit & Grace: Portraits of a Woman's Life

```
┌─────────────────┐
│                 │
│     GOD'S       │
│    PEOPLE       │
│      ∞          │
│                 │
 \               /
  \             /
   \           /
    \         /
     _____/
```

S ome occupations cannot exist in isolation. The speaker needs an audience; the shepherd needs sheep; and a pastor needs people to minister with and among. Here, some glimpses of those people . . .

The family home

You are members of God's family. We are his house, built on the foundation of the apostles and the prophets. And the cornerstone is Christ Jesus himself.

Ephesians 2:19b-20, NLT

Who says the church is not a building?

[Most] parishioners feel themselves to be out of their depth in expressing doctrinal preferences. As long as they're not confronted with flaming heresies (questioning the divinity of Christ, assailing the omnipotence of the Almighty, extending morning worship past the opening kickoff), they betray a deep-seated insecurity in voicing opinions on the kinds of debates over which saints of earlier generations would have gleefully started shooting wars and inquisitions and building-ownership proxy fights. . . .

At the same time, these same congregants are deeply invested in the fellowship to which they belong. They want to feel that they control the destiny of their church. Where, then, are their needs for ownership manifested? In matters palpable and visible. I may not know double predestination from Dutch cheese, but I know ugly landscaping when I see it.

Karl Beck, Pastor Karl's Rookie Year

By grace . . .

Heaven goes by favor. If it went by merit, you would stay out, and your dog would go in.

Mark Twain

And the scriptural basis . . .

Laytham Fitch, a retired teacher, remembers the days back when schoolteachers were allowed to read ten verses of Scripture and offer a short prayer to start the school day. He said that one day a Nazarene pastor's son raised a question after hearing the verses read. "Teacher, do you think animals go to heaven?" the boy asked.

"We'll think about that," the teacher hedged.

"*I* think they will," the lad persisted.

Wanting to stimulate conversation, Fitch asked the boy to explain his reasoning. The lad's response made sense: "Well, Jesus said, 'Go ye into all the world and preach the gospel to every creature.' "

William Woughter

The pastor's wife, c. 1600

The Parson is very exact in the governing of his house, making it a copy and model for his Parish. He knows the temper, and pulse of every person in his house, and accordingly either meets with their vices, or advanceth their virtues. His wife is either religious, or night and day he is winning her to it. Instead of the qualities of the world, he requires only three of her; first, a training up of her children and maids in the fear of God, with prayers, and catechizing, and all religious duties. Secondly, a curing, and healing of all wounds and sores with her own hands; which skill either she brought with her, or he takes care she shall learn it of some religious neighbor. Thirdly, a providing for her family in such sort, as that neither they want a competent sustentation, nor her husband be brought in debt.

George Herbert, The Country Parson

Funny, you don't look like a pastor's wife

An acquaintance once said to me, "You don't act like a pastor's wife." When I asked her, How does a pastor's wife act? she said that her pastor's wife always "just stood there with a blank look on her face, kind of like a mannequin."

I know that look. The comment surprised me and reminded me how easily misunderstood the pastor's wife is. Sometimes it is difficult when a wife hears her husband preach, to hear the "prophetic word" over the voice of the man who gets ticked off when she leaves the bathroom light on. Sometimes she can't get past the spot on his tie or the funny twirl in his hair. And she has heard that joke at least twice before.

Wendy Murray Zoba, "What Pastors' Wives Wish Their Husbands Knew," *Christianity Today*

Oops

A friend of ours, Art Bray, told this one on himself:

"The mother of a woman in our church died and I had her funeral in the wintertime. On the hottest day in August the following summer, I ran into the daughter in downtown Chicago. Without thinking I said to her, 'How is your mother standing the heat?' Her startled reply was, 'Oh, Pastor, do you think that's where my mother went?'

"Then I remembered."

William Woughter

But can you dance to it?

We do well . . . to allow a little spiritual rock 'n' roll in the church. It keeps us young. It keeps us alive. It keeps us evangelistic and prophetic. Otherwise, we might find that in excluding a whole generation of people and believers, we are excluding Jesus Himself.

John Michael Talbot, The Master Musician

Till "debts" us do part

Two congregations of differing denominations were located only a few blocks from each other in a small community. They thought it might be better if they would merge and become one united body, larger and more effective, rather than two struggling churches. Good idea . . . but both were too petty to pull it off. The problem? They couldn't agree on how they would recite the Lord's Prayer. One group wanted "forgive us our trespasses" while the other demanded "forgive us our debts." So the newspaper reported that one church went back to its trespasses while the other returned to its debts!

Charles Swindoll, Growing Strong in the Seasons of Life

Followers of Christ—or followers of a system?

The question is not, "Have we had this or that experience?" nor, "Are our views of this or that conservative enough?" The question our forebears asked has not changed nor has its relevance for genuine Christian commitment. They simply asked, "Have you met the Savior?" or, in matters of Christian living and lifestyle, the most beautiful and nontheological word formulation ever phrased, "Where is it written?"

No greater experience can be had than to walk in the company of the faithful in Christ. Let us not complicate things by guilt-producing, nonbiblical mandates whose objectives are not to make Christ-followers but devotees of a system.

Milton B. Engebretson, late president of the Evangelical Covenant Church

Like a river glorious

If you and I are spiritually alive today, it is because we are recipients of a life that came out of the grave two thousand years ago. This is basic Christian belief. This indeed is what Christian life is, and it's well to remember that Christian life can never be isolated. It is united with its source by continuous flow and is necessarily lived in participation with all who have received this mystery.

Charles Turner, Chosen Vessels

Knowing God

One day my four-year-old son asked me about God's name. I explained that God had many names, including Father, Lord, and Jehovah.

After listening to my long explanation, my son asked, "Can I just call him Steve?"

Vicki Crooks, Humor for Preaching & Teaching

Now I lay me down . . .

A missionary couple were guest speakers at a church. They stayed at the home of a widow. When they went up to their bedroom, they found that the sheets were very wrinkled and dirty. They had the grace to sleep in the unappealing bed and heard their hostess explain the next morning. She said, "For years there've been so many holy people who have slept in that bed that I've never been able to bring myself to change it."

William Woughter

Sit and keep quiet

It has always fascinated me that when we take people into a local church—the time of their greatest motivation, namely, their willingness to unite with the church—we tell them to sit down, keep quiet, and listen. After we have made spectators of them, we try to reverse their orientation to one of participation. The time to give members some responsibility is when they join the church. People need to know we're not operating the Church of the Sacred Rest.

Howard Hendricks, Leaders

The pretensions of unbelief

He [Cornelius Van Til, Reformed scholar and apologist] regularly satirized the pretensions of unbelief: "Nobody knows what is true, but of course you are wrong and I am right." The unbeliever, he said, is like a child slapping her daddy while she is supported by his lap. He is like a thief who walks into a private home, ignores all the signs that the property belongs to its owner, and proceeds to carry off the merchandise, later protesting that he did not realize it belonged to somebody else.

John M. Frane, Cornelius Van Til: An Analysis of His Thought

The chicken that answered a prayer

Marge Wiley, a former missionary to Brazil, tells of an experience that would be hard for a worldly person to believe:

"The government had built a hospital but had no one to manage it, so they asked me if I would run it. We had many cases of malaria and tuberculosis. I put a man with the most severe case of TB in a private room across from the shower room.

"Our supplies for feeding the patients were very poor, and I felt I needed eggs for this man. The only source of eggs was the chickens running around the village. When they cackled, they announced an egg had been laid. The children of the village were much faster than I, and I was too busy to chase chickens, so I was unable to get any eggs.

"I prayed and asked God to send us some eggs for this man. Later that day a chicken flew in an open window and laid an egg on a grille in the shower room floor.

"Every day after that the chicken flew in and laid another egg. The day the man died, the chicken stopped coming."

William Woughter

Keep the light shining

Jesus, our Master, do meet us while we walk in the way so that, following your light, we may keep the way of righteousness, and never wander away into the darkness of this world's night, while you are shining within us.

Mozarabic Rite

And in the end . . .

Sometimes in the early evening, I go to my library and sit in my rocking chair and meditate on things eternal. I think of what it will be like to meet Jesus Christ face to face. Then the words of Thomas à Kempis come to mind: "Of a surety, at the Day of Judgment, it will be demanded of us, not how well we have spoken, but how holily we have lived."

I have one desire.

After I've attended my last meeting and preached my last sermon, written my last book and answered my last letter, told my last joke and said my last good-bye, and I wake up in the presence of my Lord, I want to be able to say to Him what Jesus said when He came to the end of His earthly ministry: "I have glorified You on the earth. I have finished the work which You have given me to do" (John 17:4, NKJV).

Warren Wiersbe, Be Myself

William R. Woughter pastored Wesleyan churches in New York, Pennsylvania, and Michigan for many years. His long experience in the Lord's work inspired many of these stories, which he also collected from fellow clergy. He and his wife, Marjorie, are the parents of three grown children and now live in retirement in Florida.